D1177796

CALIFORNIA CARAVAN

California Caravan

The 1846 Overland Trail Memoir of
Margaret M. Hecox

Edited and with Introduction
by
Richard Dillon

▼

San José, California — 1966

Published by
HARLAN-YOUNG PRESS
P. O. Box 908
San Jose, California 95106

Dedicated to the
Pioneers
who wintered at the
Santa Clara Mission
1846-47

CONTENTS

▼

ILLUSTRATIONS

7

ADNA A. HECOX

From the Theron Fox Collection

INTRODUCTION

Bernard DeVoto's 1846 was, indeed, a year of decision. It was also a year of tragedy for many Americans who set out, overland, for the Promised Land called Alta California. The most gripping—and horrifying—story of that year's great migration was that of the Donner Party. But most of the emigrant companies planned better than the Donners, worked together better, and fared much better. One such company was that led by Captain Charles Imus, a Black Hawk War veteran. Little is known about Imus, who died in Santa Cruz in 1856, other than that he and his son (or, possibly, nephew) Charles A. Imus, eventually settled down on the San Joaquin River as cattlemen after serving in Fremont's California Battalion in the Mexican War. At least three persons in his party are better-known than the New York-born captain, himself—Joseph Aram, Adna A. Hecox, and the latter's wife, Margaret M. Hecox. A major reason for this is that all three wrote reminiscences of their adventures on the Overland Trail. Best-known of the trio is Aram. In fact, George Stewart in his *California Trail* refers to the Imus Party as the "Aram Company" and Mary Bowman in an article, "The Pre-Discovery of Gold," in Charles F. Lummis's *Land of Sunshine* magazine

9

(April 1895), wrote of the "Aram-Isbell Party," giving a share of the command to Dr. Isaac Chauncey Isbell, who journeyed west with Imus and Aram. Mrs. Hecox states that both Imus *and* Aram served as captain, or wagonmaster.

Aram's star did not really begin to soar until after his arrival in California. He won the title "Captain" before his name not on the plains but when he mustered a company of volunteers for the defense of Santa Clara in the winter of 1846-47. Aram then helped the Army and Navy with supplies in Monterey in 1847, mined near Hangtown (Placerville) in 1848 and on the Tuolumne the next year, and served as a delegate from San José to the Constitutional Convention at Monterey. He was next elected to the first State Legislature, then to the San José City Council, and, eventually, was appointed a trustee of the University of the Pacific. He pioneered the nursery business in California, with stock from Ohio, and in 1882 built himself a fine residence in San José, garnishing it with gardens of flowers and ornamental trees.

Doctor Isbell enlisted as a surgeon with Fremont's command after the Imus Party reached California, and marched south with the Pathfinder from Santa Clara but made it only as far as the Salinas River before he came down with "emigrant fever," or typhoid pneumonia, with its drastic symptoms, and was invalided out of service. He became the only doctor for the beleaguered emigrants gathered at Santa Clara although unwell himself. He and his wife, Olive Mann Isbell, acting as his nurse and pharmacist, dispensed an average of 100 doses of medicine every day. During the tense days of the Battle of Santa Clara Mrs. Isbell not only helped her husband by dressing the wounds of two U. S. Marines but also cleaned rifles and moulded bullets in the Mission, as those inside awaited a Mexican attack which never came. When Lt. Marsden of the Marines needed a white cloth for a flag of truce, Mrs. Isbell gave him her wedding handkerchief.

The Isbells later settled on a stock ranch eight miles north of Stockton on the trail from San José to Sutter's Fort, though the Doctor, like his comrades of the trail, was stung by the gold bug and formed the Stockton Trading Company and set up a trading post at the Weaverville diggins.

We know much more about Adna and Margaret Hecox than we do about Captain Imus, although Hecox's biography (San Francisco, Wallace W. Elliott, 1879) is one of the great rarities of California, not being found in either the Bancroft Library or the California State Library and seldom captured even by bibliographers. He also wrote a memoir for the *San José Pioneer* of April 7, 1878 and was the subject of a piece in the *Grizzly Bear* of December, 1911. He had a long and distinguished career before the Stars and Stripes sagged to halfmast on March 17, 1883, at the Santa Cruz Lighthouse, to signal his passing at the age of 77 years. The Editor of the *San José Pioneer* wrote in the obituary of this '46er who became Santa Cruz's first lighthouse keeper: "His end was as calm and peaceful as are the silent waters of Monterey Bay at low tide." Margaret Hecox lived until January 18, 1908, passing away at Santa Cruz, also.

Adna Hecox was born at Grosse Ile, near Detroit, on January 26, 1806, of Revolutionary War stock. His father was a surveyor for Robert Morris in New York and was wiped out, financially, by the War of 1812. In February 1829, Adna Hecox married and moved to St. Joseph County, Michigan, but his wife died of cholera. He remarried on July 10, 1836, wedding Margaret Hamer of Watsontown, Northumberland County, Pennsylvania, the author of the narrative which follows this introduction. In March 1838, the Hecox family moved to Apple River, Illinois, where Adna worked as a carpenter and lead miner.

Although H. H. Bancroft has little to say of him in his "Pioneer Register," Hecox's role in early California history was not inconsequential. Once in the state, he built a sawmill at Soquel; worked as a carpenter and builder; constructed the first native-born billiard table in California; and so earned the respect of his fellow men that they bestowed on him the title of Judge. Judge Hecox caught the gold fever, like his friends, and prospected near Hangtown in '48 but returned to Santa Cruz by July of that year. In 1849 he became Alcalde of that town and later (1852-54) served two terms as Justice of the Peace. In 1861-63 he was County Treasurer and he was appointed Keeper when the Santa Cruz Light was established in 1870. He served in that capacity for thirteen years, until death claimed him. However, Hecox was most famous for preaching the first Protestant sermon in California — unless Chaplain Fletcher beat him to it at Drakes Bay in Marin County, in 1579.

If Joseph Aram's memory can be trusted (and there are historians who discredit him), the Imus Party met with many Indians and with enough frontier figures to people one of Erastus Beadle's Dime Novels, starting with mountain men Kit Carson and old Caleb Greenwood, moving on to James D. Savage, later the White King of the Tulareño Indians, and to Lansford Hastings, the much-damned trailblazer. Others the party met included Chief Truckee, John C. Fremont, and one of the Robidoux clan. Perhaps Aram's advanced age, 86 years, when he wrote his reminiscence, "Across the American Continent In a Caravan," for the *Journal of American History* in 1907 was responsible for the errors which crept into the story. Small wonder that some Western historians have doubted Aram. He claimed Kit Carson was the party's guide, then changed his mind (without any explanation) and gave, correctly, Caleb Greenwood as the pilot. He confused the Sauks with the Sioux; and his friend, James Tompkins Watson, who wrote an introduction to his memoir, confused the Yuba with the *Yalu* River!

The volume in hand is important in that it tends to establish and corroborate many of the incidents and adventures of the Imus Party which, while they did not suffer the harrowing experiences of the Donner-Reed-Breen group, did not have an easy time of it. Mrs. Hecox first recalled her trip overland to Marie Valhasky in 1892, when she was 76, and the *Overland Monthly* ran the account in two installments, in May and June, with much detail on her childhood in Pennsylvania. She was interviewed later by the well-known Saratoga conservationist, wild-flower lover, and local historian, Bertha M. Rice, who intended to use the narrative as a chapter in a book, *Pioneer Mothers of California,* which she planned circa 1903-04 but which was never published. The material which follows this foreword is this second account, in print for the first time. It varies a good deal from the Valhasky version.

The Imus Party set out from Illinois and traveled southwest across Iowa in what must have been one of the rainiest Mays on record. They overtook the straggling Mormon migration of that year and passed them, earning a good deal of hostility from frontier settlers who mistook them for Saints. Just beyond the Mormon rendezvous, Jim Savage, the Squaw Man of the Fresno River, and re-discoverer of Yosemite, joined them. From St. Joe and the Missouri River the company, now consisting of some twenty wagons, crossed the Indian Territory, meeting, successively, Sauks and Foxes, thieving Pawnees (outbluffed by Robidoux), Sioux, Bannocks, Cheyennes, Nevada Diggers or Paiutes, and Shoshones. From Fort Laramie and the Platte to the Sweetwater they followed close on the heels of the Donner Party and they rested up with them at the Green. They met Lansford Hastings, who tried to convert them to his Cut-off but who had no luck with them (unlike the case with the Donners), thanks to Old Greenwood's obstinate insistence on the safe Fort Hall Road. The Imus Company passed Goose Creek and Thousand Springs Valley. After reaching the Humboldt, some of the men back-tracked on the Hastings Cut-off for a full day, in hopes of helping the Donner Party, but they saw no sign of them and learned from the Indians that they were still far to the east and losing many cattle.

At the Sink of the Humboldt, Caleb Greenwood left the Imus group but Chief Truckee agreed to guide them over the Sierra after a raid by Shoshones reduced their stock by five oxen and forced them to yoke cows with the remaining bullocks. Scouts who went ahead found a pass over the summit, a new one, some 700 feet higher than the trail taken by earlier parties but with such an easy approach that this route, via Coldstream and Emigrant Cañons, displaced the older one. Putting five yoke to a wagon, they got their dozen or so vehicles over the summit and, by locking all four wheels on each and windlassing them down the Sierra's western slope, they reached the Yuba River without serious mishap. Either here, or shortly, at Bear River, as they were doing the washing, the ladies of the party discovered gold — more than a year before Jim Marshall spied color in Sutter's Coloma tailrace. But the womenfolk did not recognize the metal for what it was. While drying some towels heavy with the shiny mineral, Captain Aram's wife asked, "What do you suppose it is, Olive?" Mrs. Isbell replied, "I don't know, but I think it's isinglass."

On October 1, 1846, Joseph Aram and John Kearney rode into Johnson's Ranch on Bear River. The overland trek was finished but the worst was not over, yet. They were welcomed at Fort Sutter by hospitable and generous John Sutter ("Should you need any beef, just go and help yourselves to as much as you want, and anything else that I have is at your service," were the Swiss's words), but John C. Fremont, camped on the American River, urged them to make haste for Mission Santa Clara and to fortify its buildings because of the Mexican War which had just broken out. The party, about fifty-seven strong now, followed the Pathfinder's advice and hurried their dozen or fifteen wagons to Santa Clara, barricaded the ruinous Mission buildings, and formed up a thirty-five man military company with Joseph Aram its captain.

About 175 Americans were eventually besieged in Mission Santa Clara. The Mexicans did not attack but tried to keep them penned up and hungry. Kindly Ignacio Alviso, however, furnished the Americans with wheat and the mill ground all day long and even when the doors and windows were bolted for the night and all visitors turned away. Typhoid soon broke out in the damp and crowded quarters and took eight lives by February 8, 1847; before the pioneers left the Mission six more would die. Adna Hecox, though wasted and enfeebled by sickness, himself, hobbled to the funerals and, in the case of a daughter of Silas Hitchcock, he preached on December 15, 1846, while leaning heavily on his cane, the first Anglo-American sermon in California, titling it "Remember How Short My Time Is."

A collision occurred in January 1847 between Captain Sánchez's Californians and the Americans of Aram's detachment, the Marines, and the thirty-three riflemen—"sailors, whalers and landsmen"—commanded by the Donner Party exile, James Frazier Reed. The skirmishing, called the Battle of Santa Clara, ended in more or less of a draw but Sánchez asked for an armistice and ultimately surrendered. Peace, at last, came to California and to the pilgrims of Captain Charles Imus's caravan.

Hecox, as the only person licensed by the Methodist Episcopal Church to exhort the faithful, held Sabbath evening meetings from New Years til mid-February. He then moved to Santa Cruz where he preached intermittently and organized the first temperance society, at Soquel, in the state. He also lead in organizing the Sons of Temperance in Santa Cruz in March 1851 and, in 1855, the first lodge of Good Templars in California.

Back in 1845, Adna Hecox had looked upon California as a paradise, thanks to some pamphlets circulated by John Bidwell. His wife shuddered at the idea of the long overland march but admitted that only the California fever kept him alive that winter of 1845-46 in Illinois. He finally determined to sell their home and did so, holing up in a miner's cabin until spring with his family.

On March 23, 1846—their daughter, Catherine's birthday — the Hecox family set out from Apple

River, Illinois, for Belmont, near Galena and thence to the end of the rainbow—California. They had four children, Sarah, aged seven; Catherine, five; Ellen; and Adna, an infant in arms.

*   *   *   *

July, 1966

RICHARD DILLON
MILL VALLEY, CALIFORNIA

CALIFORNIA CARAVAN

MARGARET M. HECOX

From the Theron Fox Collection

Mrs. Hecox as she appeared about the time she was writing this account.

Photo courtesy Mrs. Lavista Dake

20

CALIFORNIA CARAVAN
By Margaret M. Hecox

Going with us was Joseph Aram, wife and three children and Mr. Aram's nephew, Edwin Shaw[1], a very fine young man. Then there was Charles Imus and son and John and James Taggart[2]. It was a very small train. Three prairie schooners and a company of seven men, two women and seven children. We pursued a southwesterly course through Iowa. We were going first to St. Joseph, Missouri. There we expected to join others who were bound for the same destination. We had only been out a few days when we struck the Mormon trail. These people left the roads in terrible condi-

[1] Nothing specific is known of Edwin Shaw in California, although he may have been the Shaw who died in Calaveras in 1849. Bancroft, H. H. *California Pioneer Register and Index* extracted from *History of California*. Baltimore, 1964. p. 39. (For a time, at least, he was in Santa Cruz during 1847 where he signed the Washington Pledge. See pages 64-65.)

[2] John and James Taggart may not have gone beyond St. Joseph with the party. Not listed by Bancroft.

tion. It was only with great difficulty that our teams could move over the deep ruts made. And from all appearances we judged that the 'Saints' had been having a pretty hard time of it themselves. We soon came to one of their camps which bore traces of recent occupation. The grass had not yet started sufficiently to afford feed for their teams. Young trees had been cut down for the stock to browse on; while the bark from trees left standing had been gnawed off as high as their horses could reach. It was evident that they had remained here as long as anything could be found which would afford subsistence for their stock. Our own train traveled more slowly now, for we did not wish to overtake them.

All along the way were dead animals that had dropped behind from starvation and exhaustion. They generally selected creek bottoms for their camps . . . we had another difficulty which followed in the wake of the Mormons. So great was the prejudice against them among the settlers whose homes we passed, that they, thinking our company were of the same class, refused to sell us food for our teams, or any article that we desired to purchase. We indignantly denied being Mormons. They answered: "Yes, that's what they all say, but we've no time for the likes of you." When we showed them that we had money to pay for what we wanted, they were usually won over. The Mormons had no money, they told us, but had offered to work for what they got. Many had seemed to be in a half-starved condition. While the great company traveled with mounted cannon and were bravely prepared with all sorts of firearms, they had neglected to supply themselves with the necessities of life. Starvation, the worst foe of man, against which their implements were powerless, now stared them in the face. The settlers had not a particle of sympathy to waste on their pitiable condition. But be it said to the credit of these poor people that they really were not as black as they were painted. I never heard along the way of their having committed any depredations, or wronging the settlers in any way.

At last we were in such close proximity to their camp that a halt was called to consider the matter. Their progress was too slow to suit us. Our only chance to escape passing them was to take the more southerly route to Independence, or lie by until they were out of the way. While considering the situation, we were overtaken by several other families, some of whom were bound for California and others for Oregon. We felt quite brave with this welcome addition to our number. All were so anxious to proceed upon the journey that it was decided to attempt to break through their ranks at all hazards. When we reached the place where they had camped we found all desolate and forsaken. Only a few dead animals were left. Smouldering camp fires told us that they were not far in advance. In a day or two we came upon them and were astonished at the sight which greeted us. The company was an immense one. Great numbers of miserably poor cattle and horses were straying over the big prairie, trying to find a little grass or something to browse upon. Wagons and tents were scattered everywhere. Such a picture of abject poverty as we witnessed that day I trust never again will be seen. It was an extremely pitiful sight. Their wretched animals were not able to draw their heavy loads. Their traveling conveyances were strange and various; surely with such outfits they would never be able to reach their destination. A few had started with properly-made wagons, but others were uncovered and offered no protection from burning sun or chilling rains. Some drove mules, others oxen, some were on horseback, others on foot. When oxen had fallen by the wayside, milch cows had been substituted. That was not so bad, but this is an actual fact, some trundled wheelbarrows before them, containing all of their worldly possessions. Indeed it was this particular division of the Mormons which has since been known as the "Wheel-barrow Brigade." What struck me most forcibly was the number of little towheaded "Saints" running about, shivering in the frosty air. Mormonism was evidently on the increase. It was quite apparent that many years must elapse ere the race would be extinct.

The Mormons paid but little attention to us, and probably thought us some of their own number bringing up the rear. We were careful not to inform them differently, and passed in safety; feeling greatly relieved when well clear of them, and hastening on lest they overtake us.

The Mormons did not reach California. Nor did they reach Salt Lake that year. The majority remained in western Iowa, where they built themselves rude cabins, and managed to raise small crops upon which they subsisted until the following year of '47 when again they took up their line of march westward and settled at Salt Lake.

*   *   *   *

Our train reached St. Joseph, Missouri, without further mishap, the first week in May. We remained a few days, laying in supplies, repairing our wagons and making further preparations for the journey, for soon we would be out in the wilderness with no friendly disposed settlers to help us eke out a limited supply.

On the 8th day of May, 1846, our wagons were ferried over the Missouri River, a few miles from St. Joseph. This was about the time that General Zachary Taylor had commenced the conquest of Mexico, at Palo Alto and Resaca de la Palma. We emigrants were destined to reap the benefits of that conquest on the far-distant shores of the Pacific. But we did not know it then.

*   *   *   *

Our journey, thus far, had been very disagreeable. The roads were bad. It had stormed a great deal, and we were frequently drenched with rain. Where the roads had been so dreadfully cut up by the Mormons all of us had walked to lighten our wagons' loads. Wading through the deep mud was anything but pleasant. The chilling winds penetrated our heavy clothing and made us think longingly of the comfortable homes left behind. Our greatest difficulty was in crossing the numerous streams. The banks were steep and the waters often swollen by the rains.

We also had our little pleasures. None of us will ever forget what a treat those wild turkeys were, which our hunters secured, and which we women roasted so carefully over the hot coals of our camp fires. Wild game was plentiful.

On May, the 17th, we celebrated our son Adna's birthday. He was one year old.

Our train now numbered twenty-three wagons. Joseph Aram was elected Captain. The company was divided into messes and a routine of duty was established.

Nothing transpired worthy of note for some time after crossing the Missouri. We found traveling monotonous. I cannot truthfully say that I enjoyed much of anything upon that journey; although there was much that might have been appreciated had circumstances been different. As it was, my baby was sick all the way across. I was so afraid that he would die and we be obliged to leave his little body in that strange country for the Indians to dig up or wild beasts to devour, that I hardly knew a moment's peace. No matter how strong a woman may be in some respects, love for her helpless offspring is usually the ruling passion of her life.

Occasionally the sight of an Indian skulking through the grasses brought terror to the hearts of the little ones, who held them in mortal dread. At other times a pretty deer, or a graceful antelope, bounding nimbly over the prairies occasioned the keenest delight in their small circle. I always re-

26

member with pleasure the good times my children had along the way. When not busy with other sport they played at keeping house, or school, in the big wagons as we traveled along. Sarah, my eldest daughter, constituted herself the teacher and taught her younger sister to spell all the words in the primer, on the way.

A number of strange happenings connected with our journey may be interesting. I do not remember of hearing others relate the same incidents. One of our most trying experiences was at Bugville. That was the appropriate name the children gave the place. We had just gone into camp, and were congratulating ourselves upon having secured so choice a location, when a strange whizzing sound greeted our ears. It came from over our heads. It was quite dark but we could discern what seemed to be a huge black cloud settling down upon us. The next moment thousands and thousands of big black bugs were swarming over us. They were a species of beetle nearly an inch long with a hard shell and long sharp claws and legs. They got into our hair, crawled down our necks, clung to our faces and clothing, and literally took possession of the camp. We thought for a while that the stock would stampede; but the men succeeded in quieting them. The women gathered up the children and ran to the wagons for protection. After getting rid of as many bugs as we could, we fastened the covers down securely to prevent their further ingress. The children cried most all night and were as cross as sticks next day. The women scolded and the men swore. I never did hear men swear as they did that night. I think Father swore, also, and he a preacher! But they were having a dreadful time to keep the cattle from stampeding; some had to stay up all night to watch the stock. The insects would not let man or beast have rest. The most of the swarm concluded to camp with us, even sharing our beds. We could not escape them. As soon as daylight came we hurried on, hoping to be rid of the pests, but they had crawled into our wagons and it was several days before we saw the last of them. I have always had the greatest dread of bugs or worms, and so have my children; it was inherited. To this day we cannot repress a shudder at the remembrance of what to us, at least, was a dreadfully unpleasant experience.

What about the Indians? Well, I cannot say that we had any particular trouble with them. We once met a large party of warriors who made a most imposing sight in the wilderness. They were Sauks and Foxes, who had fought under Black Hawk and were extremely well-mounted on handsome, fat, ponies. Their trappings were gay and fine. They stopped to talk with us. Some spoke English and all seemed intelligent.

One unpleasant experience I remember. It was before we reached the Platte River. We had encamped for the night and were preparing our supper when we espied a band of Indians riding toward us. We watched them with anxiety; not knowing what their intentions might be, until we noticed several squaws among them; this somewhat allayed our fears; but much to our chagrin they dismounted and pitched their tents quite near our own. A strong unpleasant odor was borne on the breeze from their camp to ours. We did not like them for close neighbors. A number of braves immediately called on the white people, offering dried buffalo meat in exchange for bread. The meat handled by such repulsive looking beings was anything but tempting, but we humored them, trusting in this way to gain their good will. The stuff was afterward given to the dogs. We learned that they were a party of Pawnees, who had been on a buffalo hunt. A few days previously they had been badly worsted in a fight with the Sioux. A number of their children had been taken prisoners. The Pawnee Indians were awful thieves. They were considered one of the most dangerous of hostile tribes. We watched them closely. They begged us for almost everything in sight. While the women were hastily preparing supper for them—an act of policy—our men formed in a circle with them and smoked the pipe of peace.

Later in the evening a dozen of the younger braves came over and offered to amuse us by giving their war-dance, requesting us to build a large fire to furnish the necessary light. We consented, thinking it would please them, but not knowing what turn the affair would take. Our young men soon had a huge blazing fire prepared, and all were ready for the sport. The performance commenced by the Indians removing their clothing, what there was of it, with the exception of a small piece of buckskin fastened about the loins. Then with spear in hand they commenced trotting or rather hopping about the fire, keeping time with the wild music. Two of their number sat in the background rapping the backs of their knives against a stick of wood held across their knees. They kept up an incessant cry of "yah, yah, yah." The dancers, with bodies bent forward and features distorted, their eyeballs flaring wildly, danced madly on, growing more and more savage in manner. Suddenly all stopped. A brave stepped forward, and striking a threatening attitude commenced some sort of harangue in his native tongue. Charles Imus, who had fought in the Black Hawk War and who understood the Indian language well enough to know what all this was about, told us that the brave was recounting the battles he had fought, the foes he had vanquished, the prisoners he had taken and tortured, and was enumerating the number of scalps which he had torn from the heads of victims. All this was far from reassuring to us. I gathered my children stealthily about me and stole away to our wagons. While trying to rock the baby to sleep I sang loudly, too, in an attempt to drown the horrible din outside. The redskins kept up their antics an incredibly long time. When one had finished speaking, another darted forward, and with body erect and uplifted spear, recounted the tale of his own daring bravery. Judging from the time it took to tell it, I reckoned they must have just about cleaned out the Indian nations and were preparing to make a quick job of the whites. When the warriors had ceased congratulating themselves upon their great doings they were cheered by their companions with savage grunts and yells. And I, a poor weak woman, sitting in the shelter of the darkened wagon, hugging my baby to my bosom, with three badly scared little girls crouched at my feet, shed bitter tears at the thought of the old home. I wondered what had possessed my husband, anyway, that he should have thought of bringing us away out through this God-forsaken country. I feared that we all were to be scalped or taken prisoners before morning. I put the four little ones to bed, soothing their fears as well as I could. I can never, never, forget that night. It was the strangest and wildest scene imaginable. The flickering flare of the campfire threw queer shadows out into the lonely darkness beyond. The dusky faces of the Indians, dancing in fiendish glee around the little circle of firelight, showed forth in bold relief. In the dim background were the old men pounding out their wild music with grim determination. Those uncanny noises ring in my ears today. At last the Indians retired to their lodges. Our men impressed upon them the fact that it would not be well for them to be found prowling about in the vicinity of the white man's camp, for they would be apt to be roughly treated.

They did not disturb us during the night, but were back again early in the morning, begging for something to eat. We provided them with a good breakfast, hoping soon to be rid of them, watching them closely lest they steal whatever they could lay their hands upon. In spite of our precaution, we discovered, when preparing to leave camp, that they had made off not only with dishes, bridles, firearms and various other articles, but had perpetrated a piece of mischief which, for malicious cunning, was unequaled; having removed and carried away with them the bolts from our wagons which rendered traveling impossible. They were followed by our men on horseback and most of the stolen articles recovered. We resolved never again to join the Indians in a war dance.

A little later we fell in with an old mountaineer named Caleb Greenwood, one of the most noted of the "Rocky Mountain Men," who offered to guide us to California. He was a valuable addition to our number.

We had quite a pleasant experience at Fort Laramie with the Sioux Indians who were encamped near the Fort in great numbers. We rested there for a number of days and were enabled to observe them closely. The first night, while we were busy preparing supper, some of the squaws and children squatted on the grass close beside our campfires and eagerly watched every movement. They did not beg but, simply, were filled with curiosity over the strange ways of the white squaws. They were neatly dressed in buckskin garments prettily trimmed with beads. They were clean and wholesome in appearance. The little papooses were cunning and the women were all smart-looking. Soon, an old warrior came over with a message from their chieftain ordering them all back to their own lodges. Turning to our captain, with impressive dignity, he apologized for their intrusion, stating that his people were allowed to come and trade with the white folks, but that they were not allowed to hang about our camps while we were cooking or eating. We were surprised and pleased at this exhibition of goodwill and mannerly conduct. Taking a hint from our Guide, we resolved to prepare a little treat for our new friends. The women joined forces and baked biscuits and fried bacon, while the men prepared great kettles of strong coffee, and with plenty of milk and cream from our cows and a sparing amount of sugar, as we had little for our own use, the meal was soon ready. Table cloths had been spread in a long line on the grass. Everything was as neatly arranged as though preparing a feast for most honored guests. All the principal men had been bidden to the banquet. They took their places quietly, but none offered to help themselves. Every tenth warrior helped the nine seated at his left. They did not act greedy. I thought they ate sparingly, as though appreciating the kindness of the poor emigrants, knowing that they might yet go hungry before reaching their journey's end. When the warriors finished eating, the squaws and children tripped forward and took what was left. All seemed pleased and we felt that we had won their friendship.

That evening, several young braves and good-looking Indian maidens came to our camp and danced and sang for us. They were graceful in movement and, dressed up in their best toggery, were pleasing to look upon. There was a degree of refinement in their actions which we had not expected to find among "just Indians," but we found that they were "just Indians," after all, and nothing more, though in many ways more civilized than others. I doubt if the savage instinct can ever be eradicated from the wild man's breast. I think not, until the race is extinct.

The next day the whole tribe of Sioux performed a wild war dance around three defenseless Pawnee papooses that had recently been captured and presented to a young squaw, the widow of one of their chief warriors who had been killed in the late encounter with the Pawnees. We were told that in order to avenge her warrior's death and assuage her grief, she meant to torture the Pawnee children for a few days and would then knock them in the head and secure their scalps as a token of her revenge. I caught a sight of the poor shivering little papooses. How I pitied them! From the bottom of my heart I pitied them! No one dared interfere or attempt their rescue. It would have meant the loss of our own scalps.

We frequently saw large herds of buffalo on the plains. Our hunters often killed and brought one into camp. We had a very exciting experience with these wild creatures. Several large dogs belonging to our train surprised and gave chase to a herd one day. The frightened animals first ran in a circle, finally making directly for our wagons. The habit of the buffalo was never to swerve from a direct course, so their proceeding was an unusual occurance. The men endeavored hastily to prepare for them but in a moment they were upon us. It was not a large band, perhaps a hundred or more. They usually traveled by thousands. The oxen were terribly excited and reared and plunged in an effort to break away. I was in one of the rear wagons where I had been called to attend a sick woman who had a baby a few days old. Fearing for the safety of my children, I attempted to reach our wagon, near the head of the train. A large cow buffalo made directly for me. I crawled under our wagon and the cow tried to follow me. I commenced kicking her in the head. But somebody's rifle dispatched her before she had a chance to injure me. In her frantic struggles this animal lifted the wagon off the ground with her head. It came down again with such force that the hind axle was broken. I, who was clinging to it, suffered a broken collar bone. It would be impossible to describe the wild and exciting scene that followed. Children were screaming and crying, dogs barking, while people were striving to get out of the way of harm. It was a wonder that no one was killed. One little boy, seizing a whip, ran up to a large bull and before he could be prevented, commenced plying it in the creature's face. He was rescued just in time by his mother or he would have fared badly. We soon were rid of them, but several were shot. We were obliged to go into camp until our wagon was repaired. We were in a treeless country. The men had to go twenty miles to get a pole for the broken axle.

What did I enjoy most on the journey? There was little enjoyment for me on the way. It was a tiresome trip. I was not in a proper mood to admire scenery or much else with a sick baby, and three little girls to watch over and care for. There were meals to prepare, washing and mending, and many other duties to perform the same as at home. My hands were full, I assure you. Dread of the savages and other dangers haunted me by day and disturbed my dreams at night. California was not as well advertised then as it was in '49. Few of us understood just where we were going. "It's away off somewheres, Mother, by the big ocean," my little daughter said. That really was about the extent of our knowledge. The country, we knew, belonged to Mexico. Many entertained hopes that California would, some day, come under the Government of the United States. We did not clearly know what we would do after reaching this land. The emigrants were mostly cheered with the thoughts of the excellent climate we were assured would be ours. Many had come from an agueish country. It was a source of satisfaction to me to note Mr. Hecox's improvement. He grew stronger every day. I said if he recovered I would not mind the sacrifice so much. We had given up so much and did not know what we would get in return.

Whatever gave my children pleasure made me happy also. They were very simple pleasures. How joyful they were when they had discovered in a creek bottom, not far from Chimney Rock, some wild currants. How much we all enjoyed them when served for our supper that evening. Later, on the third day of July, we encamped in the shadow of Independence Rock, another noted landmark. The next day being the 4th of July we concluded to lay by and celebrate the day. The children had no fireworks, but we all joined in singing patriotic songs and shared in a picnic lunch. Some spent considerable time carving their names on the great rock. This seemed to be the rule of all emigrants passing that way. I think we did not follow the regular route which led over South Pass, the summit of the Rockies, but I do not remember why. I know that we reached a place where jagged rocks had to be smoothed down with picks before a way could be made that our teams could pass over. It was dreadfully hard on our wagons and on the feet of our oxen.

While passing over the great alkali plains and deserts the heat and dust were at times almost unbearable. We often drove long distances without water. Whenever we could do so by moonlight, we preferred traveling over these plains by night. It was not nearly so hard on us or our teams. There would usually be a cool breeze, and we suffered less from thirst.

We passed a remarkable place somewhere on our journey known then as The Geysers, consisting of several hot wells which every few minutes threw high in the air a stream of boiling water. The heat in that vicinity was intense.

Another curiously interesting place was that known as Thousand Springs Valley. A sort of lime deposit which had formed a hard crust over the surrounding ground, gave back an unearthly hollow sound when walking over it. The water from the countless springs finally flowed together, forming quite a stream.

Somewhere in this vicinity, we met a large party of Cheyenne Indians, proudly carrying the United States Flag. Few could realize how strongly the sight of that banner affected us.

We had another encounter with a tribe of the Bannock Indians which might have ended seriously but for the prompt action of our Captain. Charles Imus was then our headman. The Bannocks, in all the bravery of war-paint and feathers, were seen riding towards us at a furious gallop. The drivers quickly drove our wagons into a circle, forming a breastwork of defense, while our brave Captain rode forth alone to meet the foe. Others prepared to give them a warm reception if occasion demanded. The Indians stopped and the Chieftain advanced to meet Captain Imus. He stated that his party was on the war-path, going to fight another tribe. He was anxious to purchase guns from the white people. A strong guard was placed in front of our wagons, and ten braves were allowed to come up for the purpose stated. The deal was soon made. They at once departed. I have always believed from their actions that they meant mischief. Nothing would have suited them better than to rob and plunder the train, and incidentally to secure a few of our scalps for trophies. The prompt action of our Captain and others saved the day, I am sure.

I have always greatly blamed the men of that year for selling arms to the Indians, who soon became skilled in handling them. The parties coming the following year suffered most from this fatal mistake.

I intended to mention that somewhere in the vicinity of Fort Bridger, a small trading post, we met two men[3] from California who tried to persuade us to take the "Hastings Cut-off;" which they claimed would shorten our journey by several hundred miles. Fortunately, we did not take it. This was the road traveled by the ill-fated Donner Party, then only a few days behind us. We might have shared the same fate, being so anxious to reach our destination, had not our pilot, Old Man Greenwood[4], strongly advised us not to try the route. As he was familiar with the country, we decided to follow his advice. After reaching California we heard that these men had been sent out by the promoters of the Bear Flag Revolution[5]. They had been sent out to meet the emigrants and hasten if possible their progress to this land, in order to better facilitate the designs of the revolutionists. I do not know positively that this is true. This story was current at the time of our arrival. If so, then the members of the Donner Party were victims of a well-meant but fatal error.

Our party went by way of Fort Hall, where the greater share of families left for Oregon. The few

[3] One of these men was undoubtedly Lansford Hastings, who returned with the Harlan-Young Party. The fate of the Donner Party is often blamed upon his influence, although he was not actually with that group.

[4] Caleb Greenwood and his two sons and a Crow wife had previously led the Murphy-Townsend-Stephens Party in 1844, and performed similar services for other parties in 1845-46. Bancroft. p. 169.

[5] Mrs. Hecox was in error as the Bear Flag Revolt took place in June, 1846, two months after Hastings had left California.

remaining ones followed from here a new route to California. Only two wagons, it was said, had preceded us over the new trail. The road was not bad, although not fairly marked out at the time.

It was not far from a place called Big Meadows that we met that famous old Indian Guide known as Truckee[6], who is so well remembered by the earlier pioneers. He it was who guided the Murphy Party[7] safely into the Promised Land. He was also our guide from here on; for either Mr. Greenwood left us at this place, or else did not feel familiar with the remaining country. I do not remember the particulars clearly.

I meant to speak of the Indians near Mary's River, afterwards called the Humboldt. They were of a very low order of humanity, wretchedly poor and degraded, frequently coming to our camp in a perfectly nude state. Sometimes they brought dried crickets which they tried to trade for food. One night they killed five of our oxen and sunk the meat in a slough to hide it. Our men followed them to their lodges to teach them a lesson; which, I am sure, was of no avail. They continued to plunder from passing emigrants, but thieving was the worst of their proclivities.

We passed another of their villages, but it seemed

[6] Old Chief Truckee, a Paiute Indian, served many parties as a guide from the Big Meadows through the Sierra until the route was well established. Kelly, Charles, and Morgan, Dale. *Old Greenwood*. Georgetown, 1965.

[7] The Murphy-Townsend-Stephens Party brought the first wagons over the Sierra in 1844. All three of the leaders settled in Santa Clara Valley, although Elisha Stephens, fearing over-population, later moved to what is now Kern County. Bancroft.

deserted. Further on we came across the whole tribe busily engaged in digging roots near a large creek. They gave us some of the tubers, which looked like carrots. When cooked they were delicious, resembling in taste the sweet potato.

The Truckee River was so crooked we were obliged to cross it many times in one day. It was a beautiful stream, but was so filled with large, smooth, boulders that the oxen had great difficulty in clambering over them.

The men spent several days exploring the Sierra Nevada Mountains, trying to find a pass where we might be able to cross. On reaching the summit they traced it both ways, until they found a place where they thought it possible for the teams to pass. It was a great undertaking to get the wagons over the summit; but it was accomplished after two or three days of very hard work.

Near the summit we met a young man[8] who had been sent to Sutter's Fort in advance of the Donner Party to obtain supplies for them. He was returning with provisions, accompanied by a couple of Indians sent by Sutter. From him we obtained our first intelligence of the conquest of California by the Americans. It caused great rejoicing among our people. We felt easier when we learned that instead of going to a foreign country, as we had supposed, we would still be under the protection of the American Republic. The two men who had tried to

[8] Probably a reference to Charles Tyler Stanton who was successful in a first attempt to aid the Donner Party, although he had no relatives in it. On a second attempt he lost his life. Bancroft. p. 339.

persuade us to take the Hastings cut-off had spoken of difficulties with the natives which we must be prepared to meet. We hoped that now all misunderstandings were settled, and we had many pleasurable anticipations of our new home. Little did we dream of the state of affairs awaiting us. Plenty of trouble still lurked in the land.

In the little valley by the Yuba River we went into camp for a day or two. How pretty it was at this place and, although we were all tired out, we enjoyed everything, feeling happy that we were now so near our journey's end.

The men all went off on a grand bear hunt one morning. Dr. Isbell, Captain Aram and Charles Imus killed a fine half-grown cub. We had quite a feast next day.

It was near the Yuba River that Mrs. Aram and I discovered what we afterwards knew to be gold. We were busy at our washing down near the stream, when something brightly gleaming in the water attracted our attention. It looked like sands of gold. I gathered my apron full of the shining specks and carried it to Mr. Hecox, saying that I thought it was gold. He laughed at me and seemed to consider it a good joke. This made me angry and I threw it away. I have always been sorry that I did not keep it and wait until I could have it tested. I am sure now that it was gold. It was just like the dust they brought from the mines two years later. Besides, gold was afterwards discovered in that locality.

The same day Mrs. Aram called to me in an excited manner: "Mrs. Hecox, do come here quick;

I do believe I have found gold!" And so it proved to be the pure metal. It was thoroughly tested at the time. The men marked the spot, some of them declaring that they would return some day and search for more of it; but they never did. The piece that Mrs. Aram found was about the size of a silver dime. The specimen I believe is still in the possession of Mrs. Aram's daughter. This discovery antedated that of Marshall's by more than a year. This country was in such a tumult at the time that people had but little opportunity to search for or even think of gold until affairs over here were in a more settled condition and we were out of danger. How fortunate it was that when the great discovery of gold in the Sierra Nevada mountains was made known to the world, California had already become a part of the United States.

It was on the first day of October, 1846, that our eyes rested upon the Sacramento Valley. It was four o'clock in the afternoon when our train halted on an elevation, while our wondering eyes looked down upon the new land, our future home. We were silent a moment in thanksgiving. Then from the throats of those weary emigrants burst forth a loud and long "hooray" which echoed through the hills. We dropped on our knees and gave thanks to God, who had watched over us and brought us safely through the perils and privations of the long journey.

In the meantime, Col. John Frémont, hearing from the Indians that a company of emigrants were in the mountains nearing California, sent some of his men to meet us and solicit volunteers to help reconquer the Mexicans. The natives were again up in arms against the bold invaders of their soil. Our young men left at once, hurrying on to give their assistance in quelling the disturbance. We were instructed to push forward as fast as possible. The natives were becoming unfriendly and delay was dangerous. We stopped for a few days at Johnson's Ranch because our teams were so worn out. When we reached Sutter's Fort we again rested for a few days. None of us will ever forget, while we live, Captain Sutter's great kindness to us. "Help yourself to what fresh beef you may need," were his words, "whatever I have is at your service. Let me know if there is anything I can do to help you."

In a day or so orders came from Frémont that the women and children must be hurried to the Mission of Santa Clara for protection as quickly as possible. Our few remaining men were advised to take charge of the Mission buildings, and form themselves into companies for the protection of their families. More emigrants were on the way, and soon would reach California, it was learned, so that reinforcements to our pitiably small number of men able to fight would soon be at hand.

Just before we reached the Pueblo of San José we were met by another man who urged us to make haste. They feared the natives might attack us. I have never believed there was occasion for so much alarm, as no one offered to molest us. Indeed, the Mexicans with whom we met treated us most kindly.

How well I remember our first sight of San José. Such a quaint little city it was; just a handful of adobe buildings, and nothing more. A few Americans lived here we were informed. A Mrs. Captain Hanks[9] presented each family with a loaf of bread. We did not linger at the Pueblo, but hurried on to Santa Clara, where we were to find shelter inside the Mission buildings until the trouble was settled. On the eve of the 16th of October, 1846, we arrived safely at the Mission of Santa Clara.

We found the old Mission buildings in a wretched and filthy condition. Many of the adobe sheds were occupied by Indians, others by Mexican and half-breeds, while the remaining rooms were devoid of windows or chimneys. There were no floors and the tile roofs leaked badly. These old sheds offered but little better protection than our wagons, but we all set to work with a will to clean out the largest building[10] and make it habitable. The place had been used as a stable and literally swarmed with fleas. A room was portioned off for each family by means of calico curtains, bed quilts, and coverings from wagons. Beds were made up on the ground. No lumber could be procured. As there were no chimneys, fires were made in the corners of the building and the smoke found egress somehow through the roof where tiles had been dislodged. As there were no windows we had to burn tallow candles. I had brought with me an old tallow candle

[9] Captain Julian Hanks arrived in California in 1845 as master of the *Maria Teresa*. He was a member of the Common Council of San José and the first state constitutional convention. Bancroft. p. 177.

[10] The American families were lodged in the wing of the former major-domo's building, a wing that ran westerly a hundred feet along the north wall of the fifth church. Spearman, Rev. Arthur Dunning, S. J. *The Five Franciscan Churches of the Mission Santa Clara*. Palo Alto, 1963. p. 77.

mould, and it was kept in constant use. We had procured plenty of tallow and for wicks we tore up sheets. During all those lonely months while we were prisoners in that damp, dark Mission, our candles were kept burning. The winter rains set in early and poured steadily down through the holes in the roof. A large drain was dug through the center of the building. To this channel each family added a smaller drain. The atmosphere was damp and moldy.

By the latter part of November over one hundred men, women and children were quartered in this miserable place.

Most of the able-bodied men had gone to join Frémont. I believe that about twenty-five were left to guard the women and children. There were also half a dozen boys capable of bearing arms. Several women said if necessary they could shoulder a musket. The men formed themselves into a company. Mr. Aram was appointed Captain. Other officers that I remember were Stephen Wright[11], first lieutenant; G. D. Dickeson[12], second lieutenant; and N. B. Smith[13], first Sergeant. The officers soon re-

[11] Stephen A. Wright dealt in lumber at San Francisco where he owned extensive property and was a member of the council in 1849. Upon failure of his bank, he left California and went to Arizona before 1860. Bancroft. p. 389.

[12] Gallant Duncan Dickenson, a native of Pennsylvania, had come west with his wife and six children. He later moved to Monterey where he is believed to have constructed the first brick house in California. He also served as a member of the state constitutional convention. Bancroft. p. 120.

[13] Napoleon B. Smith came overland with the Harlan-Young Party. He worked for a time for Sutter and owned a store in Mission San José. Later he became a trader in Martinez and served as county assessor. He served in the legislature in 1852. Bancroft. p. 332.

ceived their commissions from Frémont. He also sent a letter of credit, with which he said our commissary could procure provisions for us from the stores at Yerba Buena. It was a small supply of groceries that we obtained from the Government. The Mexicans would sell us nothing. We often suffered from the want of food.

A friendly Mexican gentleman by the name of Alviso[14], hearing of our destitution, offered us what wheat we could use. We had no way to grind it until a stout old-fashioned coffee mill was procured, which was kept going almost day and night. We were thankful to get this coarse unbolted flour, which was used sparingly. We prayed for blessings to descend upon the noble old Mexican. I am sure that his kindness helped prolong many lives. The natives were careful to keep their fine fat cattle out of our reach. Captain Aram offered to pay a good price for beef. They would sell us nothing, evidently thinking that a good way of getting rid of the objectionable Americans was to starve them to death. Becoming desperate, some of the men resolved to go on a foraging expedition. The Captain ordered them to proceed to the woods a few miles away, where it was known that cattle were to be found, and to shoot an animal and bring it into camp. Instructions were carried out, and the meat divided among us. Promptly the next day a Mexican appeared and complained that the soldiers had

---

[14] Ignacio Alviso, first of his name in California, came with the De Anza colonists as a soldier in 1775-76. He became an army pensioner and was granted land in 1838. He died in 1848, leaving a large estate. The City of Alviso is named for him. Bancroft. p. 35.

killed one of his cows. He was told that the people could not go hungry. We preferred to buy our meat. If it could not be bought, we must get it in some other way. Arrangements were made with this man to deliver to us two beeves a week for which we gladly paid him. These beeves had to be divided among some thirty families. All did not get their full share.

Oh, that was a dreary, long winter. Added to the great and imminent danger of an attack from the enemy were countless other troubles. A greater foe than the Mexicans made its appearance among us. What was known as Camp Fever to emigrants, but was really typhoid fever, laid many low. My husband was dangerously ill with rheumatism for weeks. We did not expect him to live. The buildings were damp and unhealthy from the heavy rains, which seldom ceased. A disagreeable odor pervaded the place. Other causes combined to make life almost unbearable to the bravest of our band. Can I ever forget those days? Oh, the horror of it all! Many were the corpses I helped prepare for their rude burial. Within a few weeks fourteen[15] of our number

[15] This number of fourteen dying during the epidemic was first quoted in Frederic Hall's *History of San José*, and also later in A. A. Hecox's biography published in the *San José Pioneer*. Although possibly subject to error, the fourteen figure is certainly more accurate than the more often quoted number of eight, which is believed to have first appeared in *Fifty Years of Methodism* by C. V. Anthony.

Light on the burial place of the victims was recently shed in an interview with Father Arthur Spearman, S. J., historian of the Mission Santa Clara. Julius Emig, a former superintendent of the Santa Clara City Cemetery, once told Father Spearman that a group of unknown graves was discovered on the southwest corner of the cemetery. These could well have been the graves of the Protestant "foreigners" who died at the Mission during the 1846-47 winter, and who were the first buried in the now long established city cemetery.

Mission Santa Clara as sketched by Artist Waseurtz af Sandels in 1842. The pioneers of this account found the grounds and buildings much as shown.

49

were sleeping under the sod of the new land. I closed the eye of one dear woman whom I had grown to love as a sister on our long journey across the plains. Tears fell fast on her poor white face, as I thought of her children who must pass through the world without a mother's care. I remember another instance. One of the more elderly women died. After we had prepared her for burial we discovered that her feather bed had rotted on the damp ground and could not be handled with the hands. At another time, just next to the place where my husband lay ill, was an entire family stricken with the fever. The man recovered, and in his need he took some boards belonging to another from which to form a rude bedstead, to protect his wife and child from the damp ground. Mother and child both died and he then used the boards to make them a coffin. When the war was over the man was brought before the alcalde, thrust into the calaboose, and fined twenty-five dollars. He was poor and could not pay it, so his team was levied upon.

I am sure that Mr. Hecox would not have recovered had it not been for the kindness of a Spanish woman living in Santa Clara. It was a Mrs. Bellamy[16]. She came to us by stealth, with the skirt of her dress gathered full of loaves of fresh bread. One day she brought me a squirrel, to make a broth for my sick husband. At another time she gave me wine. "It will give strength to the sick," she said. Hardly

16 Mrs. George W. Bellamy (Maria de Jesus Bernal) had been married in 1845. Bellamy (sometimes spelled Bellomy) had lived in San José and Santa Clara since 1844 and had been in numerous small legal difficulties. Bancroft. p. 55.

a day passed that she did not creep in among the emigrants with some little delicacy for their sick. I have never seen anything more beautiful than that woman's eyes—great dark eyes full of pity. We all loved her. I had our wagon bed brought in to protect my sick husband from the damp ground.

The menacing of the Mexicans became alarming soon after we were settled at the Mission, and the men set to work to fortify the place. They dug a trench about three feet deep, cut down some trees nearby, and with the logs made a breastwork about three feet high. This breastwork, rude as it was, would prevent the enemy from charging directly upon the buildings where the families were quartered. Just as soon as Fremont and his men marched to the south the natives in the north who were opposed to the Americans immediately took up arms. A company of one hundred and fifty men were under the leadership of one Sánchez. While the majority of the better class of Mexicans were secretly in sympathy with Americans, and were anxious that California become a part of our Government, only a few dared express their feelings until the affair was settled. All stood more or less in fear of the leaders who were stirring up the trouble.

Sánchez[17] and his men were often seen hovering about in the vicinity of the Mission and the Pueblo de San José; but they dared not attack us. Captain

[17] Antonio Sánchez was Acting Commandant of Yerba Buena (San Francisco). He later headed a short-lived revolt against the Americans. Sánchez was regarded as a kindly, hospitable man, though suspicious of Americans. Bancroft. p. 318.

Weber[18] had organized a company of about twenty men, and they, stationed at San José, and our men under the leadership of Captain Aram, were kept constantly on the alert to foil the natives in their attempt to break into the Mission.

At one time we were informed of a plot some of the natives had concocted; a plan to creep through a court between two of the old adobe buildings and massacre our entire party. It was a timely warning; the men blocked the hole up, and watched the place that night. It was very dark, but near midnight the moon looking out between the clouds revealed dark forms skulking about. A few shots rang out in the darkness from above the old Mission wall and the Mexicans scampered off.

Some of the men were too ill to perform guard duty, and when it came my husband's turn, he was still weak, being hardly able to stand alone, I offered to take his place. As I said before, I was always timid; a bug could frighten me into a spasm. I couldn't stand idly by, however, when danger threatened and my services were needed. I knew that if I couldn't shoot straight I could at least sound the alarm. The soldiers who were not sick were almost dead from want of sleep. I put on my husband's hat and overcoat, then grasping our old flintlock between my shaking hands I went forth in the darkness to the corner of the wall assigned to me. Other guards were posted in different parts of

18 Captain Charles M. Weber, a native of Germany, came to California with the Bidwell-Bartleson Party in 1841, and settled near San José. He moved to the San Joaquin to found the City of Stockton. Bancroft. p. 378.

the yard. My oldest girl, Sarah—she was eight—stayed with me for company for about half an hour. Then I sent her in and told her to tuck the children up in bed and wait on father if he needed anything. Pretty soon it commenced to rain, a slow, drizzling, aggravating mist which lasted till morning. I knew that on my watchfulness and that of the other guards, pacing quietly back and forth in the darkness of those gloomy mission walls, might depend the safety of us all. The night passed uneventfully; surely hours never dragged more slowly. A terrible feeling of loneliness and desolation held me in its grip. I longed for the dear ones at — — — — .[19]

*   *   *   *

Mission; a man was sent in haste to Yerba Buena to appeal for aid. This was the first of January. Some twenty-five or thirty marines from one of the ships marched to our assistance, bringing with them a small mounted cannon. When within a few miles of the Mission they were attacked by Sánchez. The Mexicans were splendidly mounted and had the advantage of the Americans in that way, but they didn't seem to know how to fight, firing at random, while the Americans took steady aim. The shooting commenced about nine o'clock in the morning; for the marines had been traveling all night. Captain Weber and his band hurried from San José to

[19] Tragically at this point, a page of the original manuscript is missing.

render assistance, and our men from the Mission, upon hearing the shots, grabbed their weapons and marched off through the tall mustard intending to attack the Mexicans from the rear. But, you see, they were at a great disadvantage, being on foot while the rest were on horseback. Both parties were beating toward the Mission. The women and children, from the high surrounding walls of the Mission, had a plain view of the skirmish.

There was an American woman, a Mrs. Bennett[20], who won considerable distinction on that day. She seemed anxious to take part in the fight. She waltzed back and forth in front of the Mission yelling orders to the men at the top of her voice. Growing more excited she ran forward and grabbing up a large bone lying in the yard, rushed up to a man who had refused to fight, saying that he had no gun. Stopping squarely in front of the startled fellow she thrust the bone into his hands and shouted "take that, you puppy, and go out there and bat the brains out of some Mexican or I'll use it on you." This man quickly disappeared.

As soon as the soldiers from the Mission were discovered, a division of the Mexican force was ordered to charge on them, and went dashing at them with great speed. A volley from the muskets in the hands of our cool, determined emigrants caused them to retreat as rapidly. Again they rallied and charged. Another volley sent them flying back.

[20] Mrs. Mary Bennett was separated from her husband, Cardamen B. Bennett. She was living in San José with some of her eight children at this time. Mrs. Bennett later married Harry Love, reputed executioner of Joaquin Murrieta. Bancroft.

For a wonder, no one was killed, but a few were wounded. The fight, most of it, took place in plain view of the Mission and was witnessed by nearly all who were there. It is known as the Battle of Santa Clara and also as the Battle of The Mustard Stalks[21]. The Mexicans did not like fighting at close range and the battle was soon ended. Two of our men were wounded, but both recovered.

Before nightfall the enemy withdrew to the woods and the Americans came on to the Mission. Our women had in readiness the best meal we could muster for the hungry men. The soldiers said they could smell the boiling coffee out in the field and had hoped that the Mexicans would soon stop their foolishness and let them have a chance to get a bite to eat; as they had worked up a good appetite for their victuals. It was late before people retired that night. The Marines camped out in the mustard. We felt comforted by their presence. They remained with us for a few days, but there were no more battles. Sánchez and his men were obliged to surrender unconditionally. I witnessed the humilating scene.

The entire force of our American soldiers of less than one hundred men were drawn up in a double

[21] Grove C. Cook, who came to California with the Bidwell-Bartleson Party in 1841, was a frontiersman and veteran Indian fighter but he did not appraise this encounter as a bitter battle. He reported "the American and Mexican forces not being over two miles apart, Jan. 2, 1847, traveled all day to reach each other and at night found themselves where they started." Lancy, T. C. *U. S. Ship-of-War Dale, Its Cruises, Together with Gleanings by the Wayside.*

The State of California has erected a monument for this encounter at the southeast corner of Lawrence Station Road and El Camino Real in Santa Clara.

line just outside the Mission. The Mexicans, numbering over one hundred and fifty men, marched in between them single file and deposited their arms. This ended the war in upper California. Both parties shook hands and a friendly feeling existed on both sides. All seemed anxious to show their good will. The Mexicans assured the Americans that we could now go our way in peace without fear of being disturbed. On our side, we endeavored to impress the natives with our peaceable and friendly intentions. Most of our horses were returned to us. Many of the emigrants remained at the Mission buildings till April.

Mrs. Isbell[22] was a woman who won the everlasting gratitude of us all that winter for her excellent help in caring for our children. Mrs. Isbell organized a little school in one of the old buildings and succeeded in keeping the children occupied and out of mischief and imparted much useful information to the little ones. The rest of us were so busy with the necessary work and caring for the sick that this woman's help was a god-send to us. She had come overland with us, as a young bride. She was well educated and a very fine young woman.

In early Spring we were glad to leave the dreary Mission with its sad memories behind. Once more, in our patched up old covered wagon drawn by our faithful oxen, our family, and some others started for Santa Cruz where we intended to make our

[22] Mrs. Olive Mann Isbell, wife of Dr. Isbell, was a niece of Horace Mann, famous educator. This is believed to have been the first English speaking school in California. Bancroft. p. 198.

future home. We began to feel quite happy once more. Peace had been declared. We were still all alive and in fairly good health, thank God.

Among those who had been our companions during that long winter in the old Mission Buildings in Santa Clara, a number of families took up their residence in San José; others moved to Monterey. Among the latter were Dr. and Mrs. Isbell. As soon as she was settled in Monterey, Mrs. Isbell accepted a teaching position at the request of Montereyans.

My husband and my four children were pallid and sickly looking when we had first left the Mission. Thank God, I was in perfect health and anxious only to get our family settled where we could be assured of a more normal existence.

We traveled by the way of Gilroy and the Pajaro Valley. It took us eight days to reach Soquel near Santa Cruz, where we decided to remain for a while, at least. We were now almost without funds but the fresh air and freedom from what had been comparative prison life so exhilarated us that our hopes and good spirits increased steadily.

Never will I forget the kindness of the Spanish people along the way. Particularly the Spanish women, who came to us as we traveled along or camped in the slushy mud, for it rained most all the way, bringing us offers of homemade cheese, milk and other appetizing food. Spanish men, whom we met on the way, told us that we would be more than welcome to help ourselves to beeves, when necessary, as that was a well established custom of the country. They informed us that all that was necessary was to hang the plainly branded hide on a tree, which could easily be identified by its owner. We took them at their word and helped ourselves to two beeves along the way.

When we reached the little village of Soquel, Spring had arrived, and I never could make you realize the heavenly beauty and charm of that place. Many of its attractions have since been destroyed by civilization. But at that time it was almost an earthly paradise.

Mr. Hecox found an unused cabin in which we camped for awhile and almost immediately he secured work with a genial and well-to-do Irish gentleman named Michael Strange[23] who had an attractive Spanish wife. My husband's job was to superintend the building operations of a new lumber mill and several other men were engaged to work on the project.

These men were having difficulty in locating a boarding place. I told Mr. Hecox if we could find better and roomier living accomodations that I would gladly take his helpers in as boarders. This we were able to accomplish and it was a source of great consolation to me to help eke out the family income for we were all nearly destitute of clothes. The children had either outgrown or worn out the good supply of clothing with which we had started and I had felt forced to sell some of my own personal

[23] No record appears for Michael Strange, and Mrs. Hecox may have been in error regarding the last name. In Adna Hecox's biography published in the *San José Pioneer* in 1878, his employer is named as Michael Lodge, who apparently arrived in Monterey in 1822. Lodge operated primarily as a lumberman. Bancroft. p. 255.

garments to Spanish women who had visited us at the Mission. I needed the money to buy bread for my sick husband and children. There were no stores in either Soquel or the nearby and larger town of Santa Cruz. All of our supplies had to come from Monterey.

For cloth I found that all the material I could get was silk, satin and velvet, so loved by the Spanish women. I was forced to use such material to make dresses for myself and my children in order that we might attend Sunday services. For Father had organized a church soon after our arrival. The Sunday meetings were held at our home for some time. He also was occasionally called to Santa Cruz to deliver a sermon. It is claimed that he preached the first Protestant sermon in Santa Cruz County; and he also is credited with forming the first Good Templars Lodge in California.

There were no ready-made clothes to be had and few comforts and even necessities that we could buy.

How rejoiced I was when finally I was able to get an entire bolt of blue drilling. I immediately set to work and made the children and myself dresses and fashioned some good strong shirts for father out of the same material.

Sarah, my oldest girl, was very proud and would not go barefooted but Catherine and Ellen would hide their shoes rather than wear them until they were quite big girls. I fashioned a pair of quite good looking mocassins for Sarah, and sewed them firmly to a pair of good blue woolen stockings which I had knitted for her.

Santa Cruz Lighthouse. Adna A. Hecox was the first keeper, being appointed in 1868 and serving until his death in 1883. He was succeeded by his daughter, Laura, who held the position for thirty-three years until pensioned in 1916. The old landmark was demolished in 1941.

Photo courtesy Mrs. Lavista Dake

We wore our new dresses made from the drilling to church services. Over them we draped our heavily embroidered crepe shawls which was all that could be procured in the way of wraps. I had brought a quaker bonnet with me on the Overland Journey, and this I presented to Sarah who felt quite grown up and as she was quite a prim little maiden it was not unbecoming to her.

When the gold excitement struck us, Father was as badly contaminated by the gold fever as most men were. He went with others to The Diggins, but before leaving he first moved his family to Santa Cruz, feeling that it would be a safer and more comfortable place of residence for us, and here our family has since resided.

Mr. Hecox was one of a group who first discovered the rich mines of Hangtown, now Placerville. He and his two partners picked up six pounds of gold in one day. Later he and Captain Aram took a load of goods to the mines and cleared $2,200 on the transaction. He came home shortly afterwards and suffered a long illness. I was in hopes that he would remain home after his final recovery for he had by now secured a competence for us. We could now afford every comfort, but, unfortunately, there still were not many comforts to be secured in California. We were obliged to pay $200 for every thousand feet of lumber in the new house which we were building.

But Mr. Hecox returned to the mines again for a short time. He was able to preach an occasional sermon for the miners during this time, which some

Mrs. Hecox and her lighthouse keeper daughter, Laura, on the porch of the Santa Cruz lighthouse.

of them appreciated, I am sure. Although most of the men were too busy searching for the yellow metal to afford themselves a short recess which might have helped their spiritual if not their material welfare. Father always preached helpful sermons and he was a good speaker. I continued to take a few boarders occasionally. I was always interested in people and glad to lend a helping hand whenever and wherever I could.

One of the Donner girls, who, as a child, had passed through that tragic experience at Donner Lake, boarded with me for a while and went to school in Santa Cruz. She was a very nice girl.

We have always had good kind neighbors and I have known a number of Spanish women whom I learned to love like sisters. My children and I soon learned to converse with them in their own language quite easily.

Yes, we had a large family. Seven of our children are still living. Sarah, my eldest child, married G. K. Stampley of Oakland; and Catherine is now Mrs. Tilden Brown, of San Francisco; one of the founders of the California Club of that city. I am naturally very proud and fond of my grandson, Douglas Tilden, the deaf mute sculptor. His work has received the highest awards and praise in the salons of Paris. He is a dear boy and has worked so hard and patiently with his art, hampered as he has been without the power of speech and devoid of hearing. His talent is a gift from heaven, I do believe. God has given him the power to create lasting beauty, and his nimble fingers can talk most ably in more ways than one. He and a number of his friends, who also are devoid of hearing, often visit me. And I am so happy that I have learned to hold lively conversations with them by their own and singular methods of communication.

Little Ellen, who came across the plains with us, became the beauty of our family, but passed away at the age of sixteen years. She was a sweet child. Adna, the baby son, is a grown man now. My eldest child, little Evelyn, as I told you, died in Illinois when two years old.

Then there is Matilda, my sixth child, who is now Mrs. Frank Longley, and James Wesley, the little son who died in infancy, and Alwilda who became Mrs. Robert Riggs, and my daughter Laura, who is the keeper of this dear old lighthouse. We both love it here beside this western sea; as does also my son, and youngest child, Orville.

Yes, I will be happy to tell you about the Good Templars League which Mr. Hecox organized. It was a fine group of people and I know that it exerted an influence for good in this community.

It was organized in July, 1847. We called it, for some reason, "The Washington Pledge."

Here is the original paper, written on a blank page of our old family bible (paper was scarce in those days).

THE WASHINGTON PLEDGE

"We the undersigned who wish to promote the true principles of temperance do pledge our honors that we will not use any intoxicating liquor as a beverage. Names: Adna A. Hecox, Margaret M. Hecox, Edwin Shaw, James D. T. Dunleavey, Mary Ann Dunleavey, Michael Lodge, William Parks, Cortes Comstock, James T. Kearny, Henry Hill and Robert Devereaux."

We have always kept in touch with the growing interests of this place and Mr. Hecox, in particular, was most active in several groups, working for the good of the community.

He was the last Alcalde to serve the city of Santa Cruz before California was admitted to the Union and the state laws necessitated the election of a Justice of the Peace. Mr. Hecox resigned at this time, but continued to take an active part in public affairs.

He was the first keeper of this lighthouse, a position which he continued to hold during his life time. Dear Father, he departed this world many years ago.

Our daughter Laura succeeded her father as keeper of the Santa Cruz Lighthouse. May this pleasant spot continue to be my home, please God, till I, too, am called to the life beyond.

*   *   *   *

Mrs. Hecox departed this life on the 18th day of January, 1908. Had she lived a few more weeks until the 20th day of February, she would have celebrated her ninety-third birthday.

I (Bertha M. Rice) feel that it would be fitting to close this article commemorating the life of one of

California's noblest and earliest of Pioneer women by quoting from the tribute paid her by a young man who was a close friend and companion of her beloved grandson, Douglas Tilden. Taken from the *California News*, February, 1908:

A Good Friend Taken Away
By
T. H. d'Estrella—Berkeley

"On Saturday afternoon, January 18th, 1908, Mrs. M. M. Hecox, the grandmother of Douglas Tilden, California's widely famed deaf mute sculptor, breathed her last peacefully at the Santa Cruz lighthouse where she had resided for nearly forty years, her husband being the first keeper and her youngest daughter holding that position ever since.

"Mrs. Hecox was one of the noblest women that ever breathed under the glorious skies of California. Her many deeds of kindness have been recounted not only in her home circle, but also by the rich and the poor, the strong and the weak, regardless of race. Reminiscences of her cordial manner and kindly sympathy have been recalled by the pioneers who fittingly and feelingly acted as her pallbearers. The many visits to her home by deaf people have always been of particular interest to her, so that we can almost claim her as 'Grandma,' as her famous grandson, Douglas Tilden, does. I was excused from school to be present at her funeral.

"She leaves five daughters and two sons, eleven grandchildren and ten great grandchildren."

INDEX

INDEX

INDEX

INDEX

CALIFORNIA CARAVAN

published in a

limited edition of 625 copies

by the

Harlan-Young Press

P. O. Box 908

San José, California 95106